5-Day Morning C.O.F.F.E.E. Devotion

5-Day Morning C.O.F.F.E.E. Devotion

5-Day Morning C.O.F.F.E.E. Devotion

dawn

DAWN CHARLESTON-GREEN

Printed by LuLu Press, Inc.

First printing, 2021.

Dawn of a New Day 365
P.O. BOX 384
Grovetown, Ga 30813

www.dawnofanewday365.com

This, my first official
printed work, is dedicated
to my grandmother,
Anna Connor Morris;
who demonstrated to me, at
a very early age, what a life
of prayer and purpose
looked like.

TABLE OF CONTENTS

FOREWORD

In Northwest Louisiana, on January 8, 1974, on a blistery, frigidly cold night, with trees ladened with ice displaying the beauty and splendor of a winter wonderland, my baby sister was at home writhing with birth pains. A very important event was about to happen, an event that would stir up *good trouble* in our family.

For most families, a new baby always brings excitement joy, and anticipation. My family and I certainly received this beautiful gift in the person of my niece, Dawn Nikole Charleston-Green.

Dawn (or Nikki, as most of our family and friends call her) always has had a penchant for adventure. She has always enjoyed challenges, and has never let anything stop her from achieving her dreams, goals, and aspirations. There has also always been something about her that made one take notice. She is precocious, charming, articulate, and in positive ways marches to a different drumbeat. If you've ever had a family member or friend so special you wished you could share with the whole world, you can understand my pride in this young lady; as she, through this devotion, fulfills what I think is not just masterful work, but a calling to share her unique insight and belief that life is better when you have support.

You ever feel like there is something you're supposed to know or understand, but you just don't quite get it? I feel this describes many of us when it comes to navigating through life, and more specifically not only trying to perceive what God is doing but also our relationship with Him. Regardless of where we might be or how we might feel, God really does meet us where we are. It's obvious through the writings and teachings in this devotion that Dawn truly follows His lead.

In her step-by-step devotional, she meets each of us where we are by providing tools with helpful instructions to use to navigate through understanding and communing with God.

In Dawn's devotional, you will hear the voices of a million heartbeats, you will feel the love of a caring God, and you will be equipped to gain incredible insight. Blessings to you as you embark on a new journey or continue on one you've already begun. It is my prayer that you will grow and reach new heights into practical, down-to-earth ways to embrace life. Thanks for choosing Dawn's 5-Day Morning Coffee Devotional. You will not be disappointed.

Anna Morris-Jackson

Pastor, Wesley United Methodist Church
Mansfield, Louisiana
(Maternal Aunt)

ACKNOWLEDGMENTS

I want to again acknowledge my grandmother (though gone to be with the Lord), Anna Connor Morris, for demonstrating to me what a life of prayer and purpose looked like. She committed an hour each day to prayer, devotion, and reading her Bible. Oftentimes this included one of her friends from the church; which showed me the importance of support and accountability, even in faith. My grandmother was very intentional about her prayer time, and nothing and no one would stop it. After finishing breakfast and prepping the night's supper, the television or radio went off, and she commanded complete quietness. I could be in the room with her, but could not speak. That time was allotted intentionally and specifically for my grandmother to talk to and hear from God. There, in her bedroom, I would listen to her read aloud and pray.

One of the strongest prayers I remember to date was when I had my first seizure at five years old. It was like an out-of-body experience for me. I couldn't control anything, but I was aware of what was happening around me. I remember hearing my young mother crying in fear and helplessness; but what I remember most was hearing my grandmother…PRAYING. And then the seizure stopped.

Though I would go on to have epileptic seizures for five more years, I believe it was my grandmother's prayers that ignited my healing; and it was also that experience that strengthened my mother's prayer life and her walk with the Lord. Those present and consistent examples shaped the woman in Christ I am today.

My mother, Lynda Spivey, to whom I also dedicate this devotion, taught me the strength of a woman. Her example and her push to never let me settle is what continues to drive me beyond my comfort zone today. She would say, "I'm not gonna raise you to be sorry." Thank you, Momma…for never letting up and pushing me to strive for better in everything.

Additionally, I want to thank my aunt, Pastor Anna Morris Jackson for setting the example for strength in purpose, marriage, and ministry;
and for also writing the forward for this devotional and helping with proofreading. Your background and experience as a retired English teacher and pastor more than qualify you to be my unpaid executive

assistant. LOL! Just kidding. Unless you want to.

I would also like to acknowledge my support system along the way: Wilhelmina Bagsby (my BFF), Lenay Bolden (impromptu prayer warrior), Gamellia Davis (accountability partner), and the ministry team of Christ Church of Grovetown GA where I accepted my calling to ministry under the pastoral leadership of Pastors Jim and Connie Nicholson.

Additionally, I want to give a special THANK YOU to Stephanie "Godlywood Girl" Rodnez for her mentorship; my Jamaican/Canadian friend, Yasheika Turner for helping me through the publishing process; and Jamiah Davis for patiently sitting with me through my final edits.

But my acknowledgements would not be complete without acknowledging my covering - my husband, Pastor Leon J. Green, Jr. Thank you for praying over me and all of our children (Leon III, Shatira, Rudy, Gabrielle, Taylor, and Anasia) every morning as you head out to work. Your prayers and support (spiritually, emotionally, and financially) are why this is possible.

INTRODUCTION

My Sister, I am so thrilled to join you in Devotion and Prayer time for the next 5 days.

Can I offer you a little COFFEE? No, not the drinking kind; but rather, the being kind. Let me explain what I mean. My name is Dawn, like the morning. More formally, I'm Dawn Charleston-Green, the Founder and Creator of *Dawn of a New Day 365,* a movement for women journeying through everyday life - the good, bad, unexpected, and the ugly; overcoming with TRUTH and TRANSPARENCY, which leads to TRANSFORMATION.

Through Dawn of a New Day 365 Life Blog, I share my life experiences and try to create content in a way that not only encourages other women, but also brings normalcy to the everyday occurrences of women's lives that have traditionally brought guilt or shame. By being transparent about life's trials, challenges and disappointments, I hope to give women freedom to share their stories and experiences in a safe and compassionate environment; to live their best lives and to help each other through their testimonies.

Aside from creating DND365, I am also the visionary behind C.O.F.F.E.E., because what goes better with "dawn" than coffee? Ironically though, I'm not a big coffee drinker. I'd much rather be like COFFEE than to drink it. By that I mean, I'd rather be a *Chick of Faith, Focused Encouraged & Empowered.* Just like drinking coffee brings strength and energy to the dawn of one's day, being COFFEE does the same, but lasts longer.

When thinking about the temporary fulfillment of drinking coffee, in life, we can sometimes try to turn to temporary fillers to provide us with happiness like: money, possessions, people, things, or events. As women, we have to be able to maintain our assurance and confidence in who God called us to be when the tests and trials of life try to break us;

and when we find that all those temporary fillers actually bring us no satisfaction. But just like the pick-me-up of coffee doesn't last all day, staying in a positive and strong mindset is sometimes hard to keep too. Sometimes we have to be reminded.

If you can relate and could use some reminders to help boost or revive your faith, this is just the devotion for you.

A NOTE FROM DAWN

My Intent as DAWN for writing this devotion

Dawn means the first break of light after prolonged darkness. But understand this, at night is not the only time people experience darkness. At any time, our days can be filled with brokenness, disappointments, and uncertainties that equate to darkness in our lives. Through this devotion, as well as through whatever else God gives me to create, I want to bring my light to those in darkness and help restore women to the light of God's love.

I wrote this devotion with the intent of helping women develop and deepen their faith walk; providing both a method and a message for those who are new to daily devotions or those who need help strengthening the habit. Also, I hope to help those needing peace and clarity in life, as I delve into understanding and expecting God's peace, strength, joy, and love while seeking His presence daily with intentionality.

As previously mentioned, at dawn is usually when people get their coffee; so, this Dawn wants to remind women that, rather than just drinking coffee, we can be COFFEE and continue to have light and strength even in dark times. Our source of strength has no end. It comes from the Lord (Psalm 121:2); and "GREATER is He who is in you than he that is in the world" (1 John 4:4). If you believe that and you want to work on or continue to strengthen your faith, let's hit the spiritual gymnasium and work some things out. Are you ready?

TESTIMONIALS

Here are the testimonials from some who received advanced copies of the devotion, as a bonus for purchasing the COFFEE Collection T-shirt.

These ladies had a first-hand look and provided valuable feedback about the devotion's content, as well as elements that would make the experience better for those to follow. Check out what *Tonia* and *Lainie* had to say.

Morning C.O.F.F.E.E Daily Devotional has been such a blessed devotional read. Each day opened me up to refreshing insight as I allowed the Word of God to minister and confirm some things that I was praying about and needed to hear God's voice. From Day 1 of God's Presence, spending those first minutes of my day with God helped direct the trajectory of my day; and I continued to reflect on the devotional and scriptures throughout the day. The other four days did not fall short at all, but continued the journey, which enhanced and connected each daily devotional to my spiritual growth.

The Bonus devotional was like whipped cream on top of my latte and just added the "." (period) to that week's devotional.

Thank you Dawn for allowing God to use you and to share hope all while inspiring all diverse women. *~Tonia T.*

Dawn, I do want you to know that for us "night owls" your devotional topics, your aesthetics and formatting work just as well. **You have a real gift in making connections with your readers**, an ability to provide food for thought, and your style is clear and joyful even while contemplating tough topics. As a friend who has always loved your energy and life-loving spirit, I could hear your voice as I read each devotion. **God's love, and your love of God, shines through your words**; I am thankful to be in your "circle of women." *~Lainie J.*

God is in the midst of her, she shall not be moved; God shall help her, just at the break of

DAWN

~Psalms 46:5~

PREPARING TO DEVOTE TIME TO GOD

Either before you begin your devotion time or during (depending on whether you can actively read and concentrate with sound in the background), *put on some soft worship music* to help you create an atmosphere to meet with God.

The Bible says, *"God inhabits the praises of His people" (Psalm 22:3).*

The music will help you strip off whatever things might distract your attention and thoughts, and put you in a mindset for receiving from God's instruction.

Have all your materials handy; which may include: a journal or notebook, pen, a highlighter, your Bible, and even access to do additional research (i.e. access to Google, a Bible Concordance, other biblical references, etc.). Research and cross-referencing help to provide further insight and understanding into what is being studied.

Before you begin reading your devotional, *say a simple prayer* to ask God to bless this time being created. Ask for Him to meet you and make clear His word and instructions, asking Him to give you courage and discipline to receive and walk in whatever revelation or clarity is given.

Next, you'll want to *read the devotion*, as well as the supporting scriptures. The devotion will include a *topic lesson, supporting scriptures, and a space to write reflections and goals*. Make sure to write down what you've gathered from the lesson, how it is significant, and how you will apply it to your life. Writing this down helps to hold you accountable, and helps you to retain the information for later when you might need it for yourself or to help someone else.

Aside from reading the lesson, note that it is important to read the supporting scriptures; as the devotions, though helpful, are taken from my opinions and my experiences. God's word is forever. Through prayer and communion with Him, God is able to illumine His word to speak directly to you. So don't just take my word for it…take His.

Finally, just as you began, *close in prayer*. There is one provided for you at the end of each lesson, but feel free to go further if you would like. The prayer is specific to the lesson; and it is also a guide to help you, if you are not yet comfortable with praying alone.

HOW TO GET THE MOST OUT OF THIS DEVOTION

I've written this devotion to encourage and support the habit of communing with God daily and becoming more familiar with scripture. It's not only written to help the new believer, but also those desiring to develop a deeper and more disciplined faith walk. It's also written for those who may currently feel discouraged and separated from God; feeling as though His voice is either unclear or silent.

The Bible says, "Thy word have I hidden in my heart that I might not sin against thee." (Psalm 119:11)

God's word must be saturated in our hearts, so that when the enemy comes, we'll be able to recall those words to give us authority over the situation. For it is written, "God's word will not return to him void. It will accomplish what He sent it to do." (Isaiah 55:11)

To get the most from this devotion, I suggest always dating the experience; so that you have a ledger of when you asked God to help you, and/or an account for where you may have been in your life and mindset. Later you will be able to reflect back on it to see how God has moved in your life, and how you have grown.

Next, just like when you started, close out your daily devotion time with a prayer. Your prayer should be related to the daily topic and include any pressing concerns on your heart related to you or those God has entrusted to you in your relationships.

It may help to have situations and people already written down, so you can remember and be accountable for who to include in your prayers. This may include family, friends, co-workers (liked and disliked), finances, obstacles, peace, safety. Your list should grow as you become more comfortable. The Holy Spirit will also lay people and situations on your heart as you study. Harken to its beckoning.

So, if you are ready to get started, let's dive right in.

Moses replied, "If you do not go with us, don't make us leave this place. ~Exodus 33:15~

Start TODAY in God's PRESENCE

Whether starting a new devotion or just starting your day, it is so important to begin your day in God's presence; seeking His guidance and instruction all along the way. Never take this for granted, My Sister. Life happens…and it happens quick.

Let me ask you something. If outside of your house, you knew there was someone looking for you…to hunt you down and make your day a living hell...would you take precautions?

Seriously! If you knew someone wanted to destroy your hopes, your marriage, your children's futures, and your other relationships…would you be on guard?

Of course you would! You're too smart to get caught unprepared, right?!

Well, know this…that enemy is real and he's after you and everything attached to you. So, prepare yourself, My Sister. Be on guard against the enemy. He's on his job to "kill, steal, and destroy" (John 10:10). This has been Satan's resume' for over two thousand years, and he's not job hunting. He's just looking for new and REPEAT clients.

So, begin TODAY (and every day) in God's presence. He wants to help you. Remember, He's already seen the activities of today and wants to strengthen you and guide you through it.

There is a scripture that may be familiar to you from Psalms 118:24 (KJV), which says, "This is the day which the Lord hath made; we will rejoice and be glad in it." Notice it says, this is the 'THE DAY' the Lord has made and not just 'A DAY' the Lord made. This tells me it was intentional for YOU to be in it. There is a place of purpose for you in this day. Don't take it lightly, My Sister.

This is a day that you have never seen before and you won't see again. And if that's not enough, know that there were some people from yesterday who didn't see today and others who won't witness this day end.

This day was made for YOU and with YOU in mind; so, REJOICE and be GLAD in it.

1

TODAY, My Sister, be intentional about seeking God's presence. Let Him walk with you and guide you. Ask Him for His strength and His protection as you go about this day. Remember, as soon as you get started, the enemy is going to try to deter you from something. Don't let him have the upper hand. Let Him know your Father is with you. That alone changes the game. You've come with your coach.

Alright, My Sister! Go forth WITH GOD and be GREAT!

DAY 1 DAILY SCRIPTURES

Proverbs 3:5-6 (KJV)

"Trust in the Lord with all thine heart; and lean not unto thine own understanding. 6 In all thy ways acknowledge him, and he shall direct thy paths."

Ephesians 6:10-13 (GNT)

"Finally, build up your strength in union with the Lord and by means of his mighty power. 11 Put on all the armor that God gives you, so that you will be able to stand up against the Devil's evil tricks. 12 For we are not fighting against human beings but against the wicked spiritual forces in the heavenly world, the rulers, authorities, and cosmic powers of this dark age. 13 So put on God's armor now! Then when the evil day comes, you will be able to resist the enemy's attacks; and after fighting to the end, you will still hold your ground."

DAY 1 REFLECTIONS & GOALS

DAY 1 PRAYER

Lord, I recognize that TODAY is the day You made with ME in mind; so let me continually rejoice and be glad in it (Psalms 118:24). Forgive me for those times that I took my days for granted and was not thankful. Forgive me for when I took for granted the need to pray for Your guidance, and to ask Your protection for me and those who You've entrusted to my care.

I know there is nothing that will happen today that you cannot handle; so I cast my cares on You because Your word says that you care for me (1 Peter 5:7). Let me continue to feel Your presence with me throughout this day; and if at any time I feel discouraged, don't feel like you're near, or feel tempted by the enemy, let me intentionally draw nearer to You (James 4:7-8).

I thank you for blessing me, and I honor you. In Jesus' name, Amen!

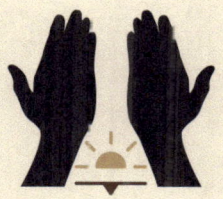

...for the joy of the Lord
is your strength

~Nehemiah 8:10~

Start TODAY Believing in God's JOY for Your Strength

Do you ever feel like sometimes you begin your day already tired? Already thinking about all the tasks that lie ahead of you because you received that text message, or you read the email that came in the middle of the night? Now, all of a sudden you can't rest. You're thinking about the job...the husband...the children...the project...Ministry responsibilities...school...what you're cooking for dinner...

It doesn't take long to become consumed and overwhelmed with the affairs of life. But no matter what it is, My Sister, God promises you STRENGTH. You just have to acknowledge you need it and ask Him for it.

As women, **WE DO TOO MUCH**. We're wired that way for the most part. We constantly take on new tasks and challenges. We love, help, and nurture others easily; BUT, we struggle with saying 'NO' or taking time to replenish ourselves. We find it difficult being honest with the people around us and letting them know when we're actually not ok; or, when we may need some help or a break. I often tell people that we *don't have to try to be what God has promised to be for us.*

I recently had a new revelation for the scripture Nehemiah 8:10 (KJV) which says, "...*for the joy of the Lord is your strength.*" I used to think that people were supposed to have joy just because they were saved and believed in God. THAT IS a good thing. However, the reality is, not all days are good days. Sometimes we just don't feel good or joyful.

In those moments when we're experiencing trials, knowing God doesn't necessarily make us feel better. In fact, some days you may feel like, "God! You do know I'm still here, right?!" We can be assured that He hasn't forgotten about us.

If we take a deeper look at the scripture, it says, the joy OF THE LORD is our strength. Meaning, it's the Lord's joy in the first place. He has JOY because He IS joy, and He gives it to us. THERFORE, we are strengthened.

I used to think it was my joy that I somehow inevitably had; but I realize now that the joy is God's already. It's His joy and His glory...and He shares it with me. Whew! That's good to know; because otherwise, I was failing to fulfill and sustain my own joy.

7

Has anyone ever shared something with you that looked really good? I mean, you had something that was yours, but what you had didn't seem nearly as good as what they had. But, as it would happen, unselfishly, they shared what they had with you. And because you experienced it, liked it, realized it was good for you, AND you knew who you could get it from again...everyday you were after it to get more. My Sister! That's how seeking after God and His joy should be.

Can you imagine how much joy God's countenance has on Him? **A LOT!** So, if we're intentional about being with God, His Joy spews out on us and it strengthens us, just because we're in His presence. I hope you could imagine the visual of that.

Psalms 16:11 (KJV) says, *"Thou wilt show me the path of life: in thy presence is fulness of joy; at thy right hand there are pleasures for evermore."*

Alright, My Sister! This is yet another reference about the benefit of being in God's presence. Yesterday, we were reminded that His presence guides us each day. Today we learn that in His presence there is not just some joy...but there is FULLNESS OF JOY AND PLEASURES FOR EVERMORE. Now, who wouldn't want to be around a friend who offered those types of benefits to you? Reminds me of the old song that says, "What a Friend We Have in Jesus!" That's what I call #friendshipgoals.

TODAY, My Sister, focus on remembering the importance of being in God's presence; in order that His joy might provide you strength to sustain your day. Check out today's scriptures. I encourage you to rewrite them so that they come to mind the next time you feel your joy is being tested or feels depleted. Don't forget to reflect on how you currently rate the level of joy in your life, and how you might make some changes to improve your level of joy. Try to go forth now and enJOY your day.

DAY 2 DAILY SCRIPTURES

John 15:11 (GNT)

"These things have I spoken unto you, that my joy might remain in you, and that your joy might be full."

Romans 15:13 (GNT)

"May God, the source of hope, fill you with all joy and peace by means of your faith in him, so that your hope will continue to grow by the power of the Holy Spirit."

DAY 2 REFLECTIONS & GOALS

DAY 2 PRAYER

Lord, I thank You for blessing me **THIS DAY**. I ask that You help me to go about today relying on YOUR strength and not my own. I thank you that **YOUR JOY** is my strength (Nehemiah 8:10) and you graciously are ever so willing to share it with me.

I acknowledge that I am nothing without You. I know I can't be who everyone expects me to be without You moving through me. More than anything, I can't be who You purposed me to be without You.

Let me not be so concerned about my own to-do list that I fail to do what You have purposed me to do for THIS DAY. Let me trust that You will lead me and guide me in every area of my life.

Today, I know that there is nothing that will happen that you cannot handle. So, I give everything to you. Prioritize my plans for me and give me the strength and the wisdom for the tasks and decisions You have set before me.

I thank You for blessing me, and I honor you; and I speak life and favor over my life and everyone who is connected to me. In Jesus' name, Amen!

11

And the peace of God, which passeth all understanding, shall keep your hearts and minds through Christ Jesus.

~Philippians 4:7

DAY 3

Start TODAY Knowing That You Have God's Blessing of PEACE

What do you think of when you think of having peace? Do you think of quietness and serenity? Or, maybe it's a special place that you like to retreat to when given the opportunity. Can I submit to you that even as great as those reflections may be, they pale in comparison to God's meaning of peace?

Let's look at the scripture Numbers 6:24-27 (KJV).

In this scripture, God instructs Moses to speak to Aaron and his sons; and He instructs them on how they are to bless the children of Israel.
He tells them to say,

> *"The Lord bless thee, and keep thee:*
> *The Lord make his face shine upon thee, and be gracious unto thee:*
> *The Lord lift up his countenance upon thee, and give thee peace."*

And when Moses and Aaron say this, here is what God promises to do:
> *"And they shall put my name upon the children of Israel, and I will bless*
> *them."*

Today, let's try to take a look at *peace* from God's perspective, and not from the way man describes it. It seems to me that God's blessing of peace is something that we must continually need, since God bids and offers His peace many times in scripture. The short of Numbers 6:24-27 is that we be graced with blessings in all things and be given peace from God.

Though there are several descriptions that can be used to describe peace; one, often referred to by man, is the presence of quietness or the absence of noise. What do we often say? "Give me some peace and quiet." We also are of the mindset that there is peace when there is no quarreling or fighting; or, when an agreement has been made between two parties. But do you understand that neither of these is a true reflection of peace? Even if I have 30 minutes of quietness, it doesn't mean that when I go back into the environment I came from that everything will be calm and orderly. In fact, most of the time people will ask for a time of quietness because they already know that what they are regularly facing isn't peaceful at all. My mind is drawn to the elementary school teacher who lives for her planning period.

13

The same is even true when an agreement has been made between parties in the legal sense. Just because we came to an agreement concerning a matter doesn't mean that we like each other or that we are going to be cordial and decent in all other matters. No, it doesn't mean that we get along or that our true feelings have changed towards each other. I can draw this conclusion from those on opposite sides of politics.

We also have the misconception that the presence of certain things and relationships will bring us peace. Some believe that if they had a certain amount of money they would be at peace. Or, if they had a particular job or position, it would bring them peace. Some suppose living in a certain neighborhood will offer peace. While others trust that being in or out of a relationship would provide them the peace they are longing.

But true peace is not found in things or people, because both are fleeting. Neither is guaranteed. Amen!?

Just like our scripture from Numbers (also referred to as "The Blessing") suggests, blessings and peace come from God alone. They ARE NOT directly associated with possessions or people. Many of us were witness to this fact in 2020, during the height of the pandemic; when people and things were limited and in some cases lost. Think about it. It took a whole lot less to prove to us that we were blessed. We counted it a blessing for just life, health, and strength. The pandemic helped those of us who are believers (and maybe even some who weren't) to realize more than ever that God was and is the source of our blessings and our peace.

But do you know that God's peace is what He PROMISES us?

So, if God PROMISES us peace, why are some of us not experiencing it in the different areas of our lives? And it's not just lack of peace in our waking lives; some people even struggle with having peace when they sleep. It's true! However, did you know that the Bible even tells us that God is able to keep our thoughts, as well as give us restful sleep? Yes! Psalm 4:8 explains that we can lie down in peace because the Lord alone makes us dwell in safety. But it seems that the busyness of our daily lives has begun to affect our mental safety and our ability to rest.

Psalm 127:2 really puts it into perspective; reminding us that it's vain to be so busy. Getting up early and going to bed late, trying to acquire things is not what God desires for us. The scripture says He wants to grant rest to those He loves.

Maybe we're not resting in peace because we're grasping for things on our own that are not God's will for us. He wants us to be blessed, but He also knows that we need rest so that He can restore us.

Think about Psalm 23. That's why He leads us beside the "still waters." To REST...Not so we can get busy fulfilling our schedules.

So again, I ask, what's keeping us from experiencing God's true peace?

Jesus said to the disciples, in John 14, that He was telling them of these things while He was still with them; but soon there was going to come an Advocate whom God the Father would send; who would continue to teach them and remind them of things they had learned while with Jesus. Today, those of us who are familiar with this account, know Jesus was referring to the Holy Spirit. But, He also told them He was leaving them with something else.

In verse 27 of John 14, Jesus says,
> "Peace I leave with you, My peace I give unto you: not as the world giveth, give I unto you. Let not your heart be troubled, neither let it be afraid."

Here, the scripture says that He not only left them peace, but it also goes even further and says that it was HIS PEACE He was giving them, not the world's peace. That's good news; especially since the world has never been the best reflection of peace, but Jesus sure has.

But why, then, does Jesus tell the disciples not to be afraid, even when they are troubled?

I infer that Jesus told the disciples not to be afraid because He was preparing them for what was to come - the chaos surrounding His crucifixion. Jesus was letting (or trying to let) the disciples know they didn't need to be shocked by what was to happen; but rather, they should have confidence in what Jesus was leaving them and in who He was.

I said "trying to let" because regardless of how long the disciples walked with Jesus and how many times He explained to them His purpose, they were in denial and they were afraid. Yes, even though Jesus told them what He was leaving them and what would happen to Him, the disciples still were not prepared. They were so overwhelmed with what was happening to Jesus that they couldn't fathom anything turning out differently.

My sister, think about it. The disciples were actually WITH Jesus, yet they still doubted and were afraid.

I'm emphasizing this because there are also going to be times in our lives that no matter how much we pray, go to church, and walk with God...there WILL be times when we are going to be in denial about what is happening to us in the moment, and times when we're going to be very afraid.

Understand this, what Jesus was about to experience was a necessary process to what had to happen so that the scripture could be fulfilled concerning Him. My Sister, do you know that there is a process linked to your purpose and a scripture that must be fulfilled concerning you? But be encouraged in knowing the process and purpose are intended only to prosper and bless you (Jeremiah 29:11).

In John 14, the disciples were afraid of the circumstances. That's why Jesus offered them peace. But they couldn't fathom it. Isn't that how we find ourselves sometimes? We've been told to be hopeful. We've been told that "*this too shall pass*." But in the moment, we're afraid of what's going on and where we've found ourselves. We're looking for Jesus to stop it or to fix it. We find ourselves even asking the question, "Jesus, where are you?" Well, I have good news. Jesus hasn't left. He's still there. AND...He's given us the constant utilization of His Advocate - the Holy Spirit.

My Sister, Jesus has left you that same peace He left the disciples, Don't worry. Just like with the Twelve, Jesus knows what is going to come.

As you're going about your day, know that there are times which will seem chaotic and stressful, but Jesus left us the Holy Spirit to be our guide; to continue to teach us and remind us of what God's word says about whatever we're dealing with. Along with the Holy Spirit, He also leaves you His peace and tells you to not let your heart be troubled or be afraid.

So no matter what is going on in your life or what happens today, My Sister, you have backup - the Holy Spirit and God's Peace. It doesn't mean that you might not be challenged; but you're equipped with what you need to handle it. Don't forget that.

Alright, My Sister! Go out there today and give folks what Jesus gave you - His peace. You'll be blessed and so will they. Just keep your mind on Him (Isaiah 26:3).

DAY 3 DAILY SCRIPTURES

Isaiah 26:3 (NIV) -

> Thou wilt keep him in perfect peace, whose mind is stayed on thee:
> because he trusteth in thee.

John 16:33 (KJV) -

> These things I have spoken unto you, that in me ye might have peace.
> In the world ye shall have tribulation: but be of good cheer; I have
> overcome the world!

DAY 3 REFLECTIONS & GOALS

DAY 3 PRAYER

Today, Lord, help me to walk in the light of Your peace. May Your very presence keep me free from worry.

I know there will always be something tempting me to doubt or to grow frustrated, but I rebuke them in advance.

You and You alone are in control of all things, and I have confidence You will lift up a standard when the enemy attempts to come in like the flood against me. (Isaiah 59:19)

You said in your word that in this life we would have trouble, but you assured us that you have already overcome the world (John 16:33); so I have faith in knowing that you have already overcome whatever I am to face.

I decree it and declare it in Jesus' name, Amen!

For God so loved the world, that he gave his only begotten Son,

~John 3:16

Start TODAY Ready to Share LOVE

DAY 4

LOVE - Some would consider it one of the dirty four letter words.

The word LOVE, though it is used often, is a struggle for some to grasp and truly understand; especially if they currently seek or have sought love through the wrong means.

True enough, it seems like we should be able to have examples and expectations of love from certain people and relationships, but sometimes this is just not the case.

The reality is there are some parents who don't exhibit affectual love to their children as they should. Spouses who don't know how to love their partners. Siblings who are unable to get along with their sisters and brothers. And neighbors who are anything but neighborly.

People, who have experienced being deprived of love in one manner or another, are not just shut out of the world or choose not to deal with other people. They go out into the world and other relationships and transfer some of their learned behaviors onto others. Even onto those who have experienced healthy examples of love. However, once these worlds connect, there becomes a cycle of hurt transferring from one person to another.

Satan loves this. He loves selfishness, confusion, hurt, arguments, depression, anger.

Galatians 5:19-23 (GNT) says,

> *"What human nature does is quite plain. It shows itself in immoral, filthy, and indecent actions; 20 in worship of idols and witchcraft. People become enemies and they fight; they become jealous, angry, and ambitious. They separate into parties and groups; 21 they are envious, get drunk, have orgies, and do other things like these. I warn you now as I have before: those who do these things will not possess the Kingdom of God."*

So, the beforementioned - selfishness, confusion, hurt, arguments, depression, and anger - are all characteristics which human nature produces. These things, however, are not what God desires for us.

The scripture tells us in John 3:16 (KJV)

"For God so loved the world, that he gave his only begotten Son, that whosoever believeth in him should not perish, but have everlasting life.

God loved so much that He **GAVE**...so that we could HAVE. So then, **GIVING** is actually an act of **LOVE**.

Just as we've discussed before, God IS *joy*, and God IS *peace*. Likewise, we also find that God is *LOVE*.

1 John 4:8-10 (GNT) really breaks it down for us,

"Whoever does not love does not know God, for God is love. 9 And God showed his love for us by sending his only Son into the world, so that we might have life through him. 10 This is what love is: it is not that we have loved God, but that he loved us and sent his Son to be the means by which our sins are forgiven."

The love that God gives to us is unconditional. We could never earn it and we don't deserve it. Yet, His love, He gives to us freely. So why do we sometimes, in light of the sins we have committed, feel that we have the right to withhold love from others?

Most of the people and relationships that I mentioned at the beginning of today's devotion, who don't show love to others, probably either didn't receive love or had thwarted demonstrations of love from someone else; and that experience shaped their view and interpretation of love going forward. But just like God can heal emotional trauma, due to being neglected of love, He can heal those who inflicted trauma as well. Yes! He's the God of the afflicter and the afflicted; and He offers His love to both.

Do you realize that before Satan set his sights on distorting our views of love that he had his sights on those that came before us and also those who we may currently or previously have been in relationship with? Satan didn't just start his attacks when you came along. He's also been after those who could and can affect who are to become. So, nope, those people - our parents, siblings, spouses, co-workers, friends and acquaintances - are not our enemy. The enemy is the enemy...and he wants us all.

God calls us to love others.

Love is the first attribute to be mentioned in the *Fruits of the Spirit*. Galatians 5:22-23 (GNT) tells us,

"But the Spirit produces love, joy, peace,
patience, kindness, goodness, faithfulness,
*humility, and self-control. **There is no law against***
such things as these."

Did you catch that? **There is no law against LOVE.** So, then, let's refuse to live lawlessly. Love others, My Sister. Not contingent on how they treat you. Not contingent on whether you feel they are deserving. But because God first loved **YOU**, and you are a reflection of God; THEREFORE, you are a reflection of His LOVE.

TODAY, go forth in love. As you go about your day, don't dim your light. Regardless of what the backstory may be, you were made in God's image and so was whoever may have hurt you. We have to start seeing people and loving people through God's eyes; for what God has purposed them to be, and not for what the enemy won't let you forget. Remember this as well, when we get to heaven, God won't ask us how others loved us. We'll be asked how we loved others.

The first scripture today is the full chapter of 1 Corinthians 13, also described as the Love Chapter. It specifies the attributes of love. As you read through it, ask yourself "Am I demonstrating genuine love towards others?" Be honest with yourself. If the answer is NO, or if you can stand to improve in the area of love, meditate on this scripture and ask God to strengthen you in the area of love.

Alright, My Sister! I love you, and there's nothing you can do about it. May you feel the presence of God and His *LOVE* all throughout this day.

DAY 4 DAILY SCRIPTURES

1 Corinthians 13 (GNT) - The Attributes of LOVE

I may be able to speak the languages of human beings and even of angels, but if I have no love, my speech is no more than a noisy gong or a clanging bell.

2 I may have the gift of inspired preaching; I may have all knowledge and understand all secrets; I may have all the faith needed to move mountains —but if I have no love, I am nothing.

3 I may give away everything I have, and even give up my body to be burned[a]—but if I have no love, this does me no good.

4 Love is patient and kind; it is not jealous or conceited or proud;

5 love is not ill-mannered or selfish or irritable; love does not keep a record of wrongs;

6 love is not happy with evil, but is happy with the truth.

7 Love never gives up; and its faith, hope, and patience never fail.

8 Love is eternal. There are inspired messages, but they are temporary; there are gifts of speaking in strange tongues, but they will cease; there is knowledge, but it will pass.

9 For our gifts of knowledge and of inspired messages are only partial;

10 but when what is perfect comes, then what is partial will disappear.

11 When I was a child, my speech, feelings, and thinking were all those of a child; now that I am an adult, I have no more use for childish ways.

12 What we see now is like a dim image in a mirror; then we shall see face-to-face. What I know now is only partial; then it will be complete— as complete as God's knowledge of me.

26

13 Meanwhile these three remain: faith, hope, and love; and the greatest of these is love.

Matthew 7:11 (GNT)

As bad as you are, you know how to give good things to your children. How much more, then, will your Father in heaven give good things to those who ask him!

Matthew 22:37-38 (GNT)

Jesus answered, "'Love the Lord your God with all your heart, with all your soul, and with all your mind.' 38 This is the greatest and the most important commandment. 39 The second most important commandment is like it: 'Love your neighbor as you love yourself.'

DAY 4 REFLECTIONS & GOALS

DAY 4 PRAYER

Lord, help me to truly love others. Let me not just say it, but show it in my actions; that others may see a reflection of Your love in me.

Lord, there are times that love, or lack of love, hurt me, and left a deep scar; but I understand that love has also hurt You. We hurt You when we don't obey You or trust You; yet You still pour out Your unconditional love towards us. Help me to be more like that. Help me to forgive quickly so that healing and deliverance can take place.

I know that there may be some deep scars from love-hurt in me or in others that I am in relationship with. Lord, help us to feel Your unwavering love for us and help us to heal so that Your joy and peace might be reflective in us, and we can draw others closer to You through the love that we show.

I submit this prayer to You, Oh Lord. You know what I have need of. You know who I need to show love; so help me to be a better lover. You also know who I want to feel love from. However, if I don't sense that love or ever get it, help me to still walk in obedience to what You say about love. Let me be that reflection of You, because I know that regardless You love me unconditionally.

I praise You that You are healing my heart and mending relation- ships. I trust that You are perfecting that which concerns me (Psalm 138:8), and I thank You that You first loved me, in Jesus' name, Amen!

But my God shall supply all your need according to his riches in glory by Christ Jesus.

~Philippians 4:19~

DAY 5

Start TODAY Seeking God First Before Everything for PROVISION

My Sister, I'm gonna dive straight into this one today. Up until this point, you've been spending intentional time with God and in His word each day. Whether spending this time was something you were already accustomed to doing regularly, or if you just started during this journey; it's always a remarkable practice to make deliberate time to connect with God. He wants to hear from you. The more often you do, the more natural it will become. But even more than that, there is something that we are instructed to do in scripture that should prompt us to spend time with God before anything else.

Matthew 6:33 (KJV) says,

> *"But seek ye first the kingdom of God, and his righteousness; and all these things shall be added unto you."*

My Sister, before we do anything else - consult with anyone, take any matter into consideration - we are to first *SEEK GOD*. We are to first seek His presence, so that we can hear from Him. Hearing from God drives us towards those things that are naturally pleasing to him.

Some people focus on the latter part of the scripture that says, **"and all these things shall be added unto you"** and just start thinking about material things and earthly desires and plans. And yes, God is able to give us those things; but we need to be carful not to be an opportunist with God. We shouldn't seek a relationship just to get something out of Him; and then, once we get it, go back to our old habits.

Isn't that typically what people do? 'If God gives me this, I promise I will do that." But after we get what we want, we disconnect from God. It's almost like ordering something from Amazon that we really want. We get it, take it out of the box, and throw the box away...along with the instructions. We still have a great product, and we can use it for the most part; but we don't have an understanding of its capabilities because we threw the instructions away.

There is a reason the manufacturer included, not only the instructions, but the warnings, and the warranty option. Us using the product, without a full understanding of what it's capable of, doesn't allow for full proficiency, and

31

could possibly put us in danger of being injured. The manufacturer knows the product. The product has gone through safety tests to even be cleared to bring it into our homes. So why would we throw the directions away?

Well, if we think about it, we do the same thing with God and His word. We ask God for something we desire, but when we get it, we never refer back to the instructions - the Bible. The Bible gives us instruction on how we are to live, love, lead, minister, study, live at peace, parent, and act in response to our children, our spouses, and others.

We literally pray for all of these things - love, children, careers, status, purpose - but then when we get them we fail to refer back to the instructions on how to manage or steward them well. My Sister, that's just like throwing the directions away with the box. We'll never know what we are fully capable of or how to care for what we've been blessed with if we don't seek God daily. He has given us an instruction manual. There are safety features available to us, and we are covered under the manufacturer's warranty. When…we seek him.

Jeremiah 29:11 tells us that God alone knows the plan for our lives. Why? Because He's not only the manufacturer, He's the Creator. Not all manufacturers are the creators of a product and vice versa. But how great is it that our God is One and the Same?!

It further says in Jeremiah that God's plans are to give us a future and a hope. You know what the future and the hope are? **All those things that shall be added unto us when we seek him first**. (Matthew 6:33)

Notice I didn't say "IF" we seek Him first, but "WHEN" we seek Him first. Because I believe that's what you're gonna do. My Sister; because you want the best of what God has for you, and you want to be able to use everything He has for you to its fullest capability.

TODAY, if you don't remember anything else from this devotion, remember this - always refer to the owner's manual and you are well on your way to what God is going to add to you. He is truly able to supply all your needs (Philippians 4:19). I believe it, in Jesus' name.

DAY 5 DAILY SCRIPTURES

Proverbs 16:1 (GNT)
"We may make our plans, but God has the last word."

Proverbs 16:9 (GNT)
"You may make your plans, but God directs your actions."

Romans 12:1-2 (KJV)
"I beseech you therefore, brethren, by the mercies of God, that ye present your bodies a living sacrifice, holy, acceptable unto God, which is your reasonable service. 2 And be not conformed to this world: but be ye transformed by the **renewing of your mind**, that ye may <u>prove what is that good</u>, and <u>acceptable</u>, and <u>perfect</u>, will of God.

Colossians 3:23 (GNT)
"Whatever you do, work at it with all your heart, as though you were working for the Lord and not for people."

DAY 5 REFLECTIONS & GOALS

DAY 5 PRAYER

Lord, let me seek to make room for You in my life everyday. Let me not make a plan that doesn't include You in it first. You are my manufacturer. You made me, so You know exactly how my life is supposed to go. Only You know the exact plan. Let me always be willing to trust You even when the circumstances in life I don't understand. Help me to remember that my goals should always lead me to You.

Lord, don't let me choose a path that's not Yours; but don't let me walk in fear either. So, continue to give me LOVE, POWER, and a SOUND MIND (2 Timothy 1:7). I thank you that You love me, and we have a relationship that You never walk away from. You love me even when I'm unlovable.

Lord, let You always be my ultimate goal in life and not just my own goals or what You can do for me. I don't want to be selfish and self-seeking in this relationship. Help me to be concerned about what You think and not of what others think of me. Let me do everything with the mindset that what I'm doing is for You (Colossians 3:23). I'm loving my husband for You. I'm loving my children for You. I'm going to school for You. I'm doing my job well for You. I'm kind to others for You. I'm walking in truth and integrity for You.

Lord, let me please You with all of my being. I realize that this path of righteous is for Your name sake and not merely for myself (Psalms 23). For as I seek You, I pray to be a reflection of You to others. Make me the light and salt of the earth that you intended (Matthew 5:13-16). In Jesus' name I pray, Amen!

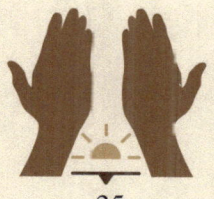

Give us this day our daily bread.

~Matthew 6:11~

Start TODAY with AN EXTRA SHOT OF EXPRESSO - For God's SUSTAINMENT

BONUS

Thank you so much, My Sister, for joining me in the last five days of devotion. TWG (Time with God) is something that is truly valuable to me. I don't know about you, but when I don't get it, I'm completely unbalanced. I can explain it best like this. Time without God for me is like being on a crash diet. Your body has gotten so used to you filling it up with food and not being hungry that as soon as you deprive it, you start going through withdrawals. Some people when they diet to lose weight experience headaches, low energy, extreme irritability, and short patience. That's just what I face when I deny myself time with God.

Apart from God, I can't focus. My energy is low. I am short-tempered and impatient. Yep! All the things people go through with a physical diet mirror what I suffer with and feel when on a spiritual one. But the difference is…with a physical diet, the goal is to lose weight in order to feel good about yourself, regain better health, or to fit back into your favorite pair of jeans. Let's just be clear! There is absolutely **NO BENEFIT** from dieting on the Word of God. When you diet from God's Word and time with Him, what you lose is your faith, peace, mental and emotional strength, and will to do anything purposeful. Then, you gain the weight of the world.

I don't know about you, but I need as much faith, peace, mental and emotional strength, and will as I can get. Without them, there is no Dawn of a "new day." There is Dawn and her "old ways," and she ain't cute. Like being healthy is a lifestyle that can help keep your physical weight under control, I want to live a spiritual lifestyle that keeps me free of warfare weight. God's word keeps us spiritually healthy and strong. In order to maintain that lifestyle, we have to feast on His word daily. That is what's going to sustain us.

In Matthew 6:11 (commonly known as the Lord's Prayer), there is a portion that says, *"Give us this day our daily bread."* I will admit, when I used to recite this, I would only think of food. Yes, of course, we want God to feed us every day. We need nourishment to live. But the scripture is actually a little deeper than that.

In the Old Testament Book of Exodus, when the Children of Israel were in the desert, they had to meet God each morning in order to get their daily sustenance. Seriously! They had to physically go outside of their tents during the time specified to actually meet God; and during this time **AND THIS TIME ONLY** would He provide them with the food they would need for the day. Scripture describes it as *"manna from heaven."* If they overslept, **God**...AND HIS FOOD...were gone. If any of them tried to get too much (so they wouldn't have to return the following day or just to be greedy) the food would spoil and get maggots in it. God's instructions were very specific, and they had to act in obedience.

God provided each of them (each household) just the portion that was needed for THAT DAY. And scripture tells us that no one who met in God's presence EVER ran out. He provided their "DAILY BREAD" every day. He gave them just what they needed.

My Sister, I'm not sure if you noticed, but God just ain't raining manna from heaven anymore. Yet, I believe His concept still holds true. God desires for us to meet Him DAILY in prayer and in His word so that He can provide you and I with exactly what is needed for our daily "spiritual" sustenance. In response to our obedience, He's going to provide the physical, natural, tangible needs that are necessary for our lives. God wants to give His children good things because He's a Good Father like that. BUT, along with the giving, He wants a relationship too. He wants to COMMUNE with us.

With our sweet communion with the Lord, He's not necessarily raining down manna from heaven anymore, but he's definitely raining down blessings. Could you use some daily blessings? Well, continue to meet God daily, My Sister; coming into His presence; getting His daily word, that He so willingly will give to you - so that you can be the best version of yourself the way He truly intended.

Answer the questions:
What is God telling you to give Him more of?
What area of your life is He asking you to trust Him in?
What's keeping you from it?

Regardless of how things may sometimes seem, God truly does have the plan for your life. Two beautiful women God is using in this season to walk in their purpose shared their hearts with me to remind me of this. One said, "A delayed promise from God is still a promise from God. The other said, "Remember, you may only see what's in front of you, but He sees what is ahead." Their words resonated well with me and encouraged me. I hope you find them helpful too. Plainly put, let God guide you.

Alright, My Sister! I've enjoyed these days of morning C.O.F.F.E.E. with you; but don't forget, our goal is to not just drink coffee but to be it — a **Chick Of Faith, Focused Encouraged & Empowered**. Know that God is brewing something uniquely special in you each day. Stir it up, My Sister. It's the gift that He has in you (1 Timothy 1:1-7). And I believe His Word that says, He can perfect those things which concern you (Psalm 138:8). In Jesus' name!

FINAL NOTE:
Know that you are worthy of His **LOVE, JOY, PEACE, STRENGTH, GRACE, GUIDANCE and PROVISION**. He makes them available to you each day. Don't leave them behind. Take them with you wherever you may go. When you enter the room, the atmosphere should shift because you've brought company.

Remember that God's mercies are new for you each morning (Lamentations 3:22-23). So, everyday wake up expecting God to do something great. Thankfully, God doesn't pack our baggage from yesterday and bring it to us the following day, and neither should you. Let go of unforgiveness, past mistakes, past hurts, regrets, and disappointments. When you look for God even in the unexpected, He'll show up in ways you never imagined.

I believe something new is on the horizon. It's the Dawn of YOUR New Day. Rejoice and be glad in it. ~Dawn~

SCRIPTURES

Psalms 36:7-9 (GNT)

"How precious, O God, is your constant love!
We find protection under the shadow of your
wings. 8 We feast on the abundant food you provide; you let us drink from
the river of your goodness. 9 You are the source of all life, and because of
your light we see the light.

2 Corinthians 5:17 (KJV)

"Therefore if any man be in Christ, he is a new creature: old things are
passed away; behold, all things are become NEW."

READ INDEPENDENTLY: *Exodus 16:1-35 - The Manna and the Quails -*
Read this at your leisure. The entire passage will not only enlighten you, but
also amaze you concerning the Power of God.

FINAL REFLECTIONS & GOALS

CLOSING PRAYER

Lord, I pray that You would give me Your discipline daily to remain in Your word. Let me make room in my daily schedule to meet with You so that You can provide me the daily spiritual sustenance I need to sustain the tasks set before me, the relationships You've entrusted to me, and the purpose and calling that You have placed over my life. I acknowledge that I can't do these on my own.

Let Your Holy Spirit continue to guide me and teach me as I go throughout each day. Let Your voice be so clear to me that a stranger's voice I will not respond to. Let every duty, project, venture that I aspire to obtain be ordained by You and in Your will. Let me always humble myself to ask You first, so that I know what I'm doing will go well. Give me the maturity to humbly walk away from those things and relationships that You have not intended for me.

May I represent You in every area of my life so that others may be drawn to have a closer relationship with You because of my example.

Lord, bless my mind that I would have thoughts that bring You glory. I bind the spirit of anxiety, worry, doubt, fear and depression. I speak blessings over my family, my finances, my relationships, and my purpose. I trust that You have the perfect plan for my life, which is not to harm me but to bless me (Jeremiah 29:11). And I know that You are able to do exceedingly abundantly above all that I can ask or think (Ephesians 3:20).

I decree and declare these things, and I count them done in Jesus' name, Amen!

THANK YOU

Thank you so much for committing to this journey for a deeper walk with God by delving into His word for the past 5-Days.

This is a guilt free zone, so even if you missed some days or even if it took you a while to actually complete the process, you made it to the end. I learned through a devotion I did called Jesus' Calling, by author Sarah Young, that we cannot make our schedules idols before God; so concerned about the schedule that we've penciled in that we fail to follow or walk in obedience and faith to the path God is leading us through.

Nothing catches God by surprise. I am sure that whatever He revealed to you on any given day was just what you were supposed to receive to speak to your specific and immediate need for that day.

But don't stop here. Don't allow the enemy to strip you of what you have learned, or the habits you've developed. Keep going, My Sister.

I would encourage you to find a plan on the YouVersion Bible App or another online resource that speaks to what you believe God is calling you to focus on or overcome in this next season.

You can always feel free to go back through and revisit this devotion for better clarity. And **PLEASE,** if you found this devotion helpful, share it and what you've learned with another woman who might find it beneficial. Remember what Luke 22:31 says, *"Satan desires to sift you like wheat, but I have prayed that your faith not fail; and after you've been strengthened, go back and strengthen your brother"...or sister in this case.*

I am grateful to have been a part of this journey with you. I'll see you on the horizon as you await your Dawn of a New Day. Continue to not just drink coffee, but to be COFFEE - Chicks Of Faith Focused Encouraged & Empowered.

Yours in Christ,

44

ABOUT THE AUTHOR

Dawn Charleston-Green, M.Ed.
Creator - Writer - Minister - Speaker
Dawn of a New Day 365, LLC

Dawn Charleston-Green is the Founder and CEO of Dawn of a New Day 365. The Dawn of a New Day 365 movement focuses on women journeying through everyday life–the good, the bad, the unexpected, and the ugly; overcoming with TRUTH and TRANSPARENCY, leading to TRANSFORMATION.

Dawn, a native of Mansfield Louisiana, has worked in the fields of Education, Social Service and Child Advocacy, and is also a Military Veteran. She currently, however, works from home as a Christian minister, entrepreneur, blogger-influencer, award-winning self-published author, and speaker.

As an ordained minister and teacher, Dawn served for over 15 years in ministry as a Pianist and Praise Leader. Dawn is a graduate of Northwestern State University of Louisiana; where she received a Bachelor of Arts in English in 1996 and a Masters of Education in Counseling in 2003. She is 12 hours shy of her doctoral degree in Education Leadership. Dawn served in the United States Army from 1996-2007; completing her time in service as a Captain and Finance Officer.

Dawn currently serves as Vice President on the Board of Directors for Still Waters Ministries. Formerly, she served on the Executive Board for Georgia Court Appointed Special Advocates for Children (CASA) and the Augusta University Social Work Advisory Board. She was a 2012 Shero Award Recipient in Law & Government. Notably, she also holds other prestigious awards; such as the Joint Service Commendation Medal, Military Outstanding Volunteer Service Medal, and the Bronze Wahathchee Award for Volunteerism. Dawn has been a member of Delta Sigma Theta Sorority, Inc. for over 30 years.

Dawn is the bride of Retired Command Sergeant Major and Pastor Leon Green Jr. and they have a blended family of 6 children. She is her husband's partner in ministry, as together they lead the ROCK Minitires, Inc. where their mission is to Reach and Restore Others for Christ's Kingdom (R2OCK); supporting local outreach and in-reach in Georgia, as well as efforts abroad.

MORE FROM THE AUTHOR

In addition to the *5-Day Morning COFFEE Devotion*, Dawn is also the lead author of *New Day of G.R.A.C.E.* - a 21-day devotion written with the intent of helping women facing the difficulties of starting over after a setback, loss, or disappointment. New Day of G.R.A.C.E. is written to help inspire courage and hope that life is not over; but rather, on a path to a **NEW BEGINNING**.

Dawn is also an award-winning children's book author. Check out her titles:

- *HEEEYY DANDELION* - a story that gently addresses childhood self-esteem, honesty, and family belonging.
- *MIND YOUR MANNERS* - five short stories that address: Hygiene, Courtesy, Table Manners, Respect, and Patience
- *RUDY THE SMART KID* - a story about curiosity and confidence to encourage children, especially boys, to see themselves and the potential and possibilities available to them.

Find these children's books on their dedicated websites:
heeeyydandelion.com, rudythesmartkid.com, or dawnofanewday365.com.

These titles are also available on *Amazon, Barnes & Noble*, or wherever books are sold. Books are available in *paperback*, hardcover, *eBook*, and *Audible*. Heeeyy Dandelion is also available in *Spanish*.

Want to Tell a Story or Tell It Better?

If you've got a story to tell, but need help putting it on paper, Dawn would love to help you bring your story to life. Let award-winning author Dawn Charleston-Green help you with writing, editing, copyrighting, publishing, and preliminary marketing. You too can be a published author.

Or, maybe you've already published a book and need help gaining more exposure. Dawn's book and publishing strategies can help with that too.

Join the *Rising Author Academy* at
dawnofanewday365.com/author-academy/

WAYS TO CONNECT

If you would like to schedule a 30-minute after-action coaching call with Dawn, email: **info@*dawnofanewday365.com*.** Please be sure to put Faith Coaching Call Request in the Subject Line.

For speaking engagements and collaborations, reach out to Dawn on any of her fields of expertise, which include: **Ministry, Leadership, Faith, Women, Children, Marriage, Families, Relationships, Foster Parenting, Adoption, College Preparation, and MORE.**

For more information from
Dawn Charleston-Green and Dawn of a New Day 365
Subscribe to Dawn of a New Day 365 by going to
dawnofanewday365.com

Dawn of a New Day 365 is a movement focused on women journeying through everyday life – the good, the bad, the unexpected, and the ugly; overcoming with TRUTH and TRANSPARENCY, that leads to TRANSFORMATION. Join the movement.

Follow the Dawn of New Day 365 movement on:
Facebook, YouTube, Instagram, and Pinterest

Check out Dawn's latest books and apparel at:
dawnofanewday365.com/shop

Made in the USA
Columbia, SC
20 March 2024

33036832R00041